The Path Towards Sunshine

by Lorelai Symmes

To Alexis – Without you, I never would have stepped up onto the path towards sunshine. You are the reason I now stand where I am. I will be forever grateful.

Acknowledgements

Mom and Dad – Words will never be able to describe the love and appreciation my heart holds for you. Thank you for everything.

Mrs. Hill – For introducing me to the art that saved my life. Thank you.

Danielle – You have stood by me even when the seas turned rough. Thank you for being my greatest support outside of home. I love you.

Table of Contents

SPOKEN WORD..11

  Dear Thinspo 13

  1011 Days 17

  The First Time...19

  To My Sister 21

FREE VERSE 23

  New Beginnings..25

  Failure's Tone 27

  I Love You 29

  Life Is Too Short 31

  The Rising of the Sun 33

  Before..35

  True Beauty...37

  Beauty Is Pain 39

  Breath of Life 41

  The Connotation of Health................................43

  My Love for You 45

  Hold On...47

  Ana's Validation 49

  Hope 51

  Day by Day 53

  Little Things..55

  You...57

  The Treasure of You 59

  The World in Your Hands..................................61

  Your Precious Breath..63

  The House That Made You.................................65

  A Stainless Steel Heart 67

  His Words 69

  A Glimmer of Hope...71

  Together 73

The Heart Wants What it Wants................................75
My Body's Welcome................................77
Sick Enough 79
Pride................................81
Time of Life................................83
Ana's Wrath................................85
The Flight of Growth................................87
Free Flight 89
A New Place................................91
The Past Is in the Past................................93
Escaping the War................................95
Hope Chooses Hope................................97
Love Is a Suicide Note................................99
You Before Him................................101
The Truth of Starvation................................103
When it Hit................................105
Homosapiens................................107
True Worth................................109
The Middle................................111
The Power of Her Rays 113
Life as a Novel................................115
Freedom at Last................................117
When I was Younger 119
Blooming Beyond................................121
The Blooming of My Soul 123
Drink Up................................125
Scars to Your Beautiful................................127
The Curse of Literature 129
Measured Beauty 131
For You 133
Break the Chains................................135
Racing 137
Lie................................139
She, the Sun................................141

Finally 143

Change by Day 145

My Epiphany 147

From That Moment On 149

Love Doesn't Discriminate 151

In and Out 153

The Drug That's You 155

Anxiety, Anxiety 157

Stainless Steel Hearts 159

Here 161

Growth from Light 163

Safety Stays 165

Beauty from Above 167

Away 169

She Stayed 171

The Someone 173

Devotions Deserved 175

Starving Dreams 177

Home of the Soul 179

You Before Them 181

Cracks Are Not Permanent 183

The End of It All 185

What Is Love? 187

The Elements 189

Our Society 191

Grateful 193

Death of a Friend 195

SPOKEN WORD

Dear Thinspo

You're fat
Those were the words spoken to me that sparked the
beginning of an eternity
God, if only he knew that truly I would follow through
I did what I thought I should, but I didn't know what pain it
could
Cause inside my 11-year-old brain
The shame I swear was the worst of it
Hiding what I thought I'd gain
You'll never be thin, I told myself
Throw those thoughts on a shelf
Because you have to lose weight, I said
You have to be what society wants or your potential will be
dead
Little did I know that's not what'd be dead
Anorexia is not a thin girl with a pretty smile
It's not knowing if you'll have a while
Slowly, you push people away
All you want is for Ana to stay
Your hair begins to fall out
Tears flow as if from a spout
Only one more pound, you tell yourself
But one turns to five turns to ten until it begins to kill your
health
Thin hair covers your body
Dark circles enclose those once bright eyes
You need to stop, they tell you
Mom, just leave me be
Dad, I'll be okay
Sitting in a room in a hospital gown
They come in with such a solemn frown

Lorelai, you're severely underweight
Though in my mind I'm the farthest from that
Potassium, phosphorous are thrown around
When you stand, your legs hit the ground
Still think anorexia is beautiful?
Well, think again, dear soul
I am not 1 in 5
My life is not meant to be stuck in a hospital bed
The light was not so far ahead
Death still crept like a crab in a shell
Have you ever been stripped away from your family?
Thrown in a place that looks from hell
Still think anorexia is beautiful?
Needles shoved through my veins
My muscles can't withstand but a strain
Hope is lost; your will is gone
This is the true reality
Googling the calories in Chapstick
Because you are so scared of what may occur
It's stupid; I'm aware, sure
But to me, it's surreal
Do you still think anorexia is beautiful?
A lifestyle of restriction and pain
It's not some twisted game
Setting alarms at 2 a.m.
To get up and exercise until you just can't anymore
It's like a drug
That you can't just brush under the rug
Do you still think anorexia is beautiful?
Never forget that you deserve to live, not only breathe
Not slumped over a toilet trying to heave
Blue nails grasp the rail
Your parents pray the hail
Longing for their baby back

I am only 14 years old
Still not a clue if I will ever be free
From the disease that's consuming me
So tell me now, if you will
Do you still think anorexia is beautiful?

1011 Days

1011 days
1011 days since I developed an eating disorder
1011 days since my self-love withered as my body became
smaller and smaller
1011 days filled with weekly appointments and too many
tears
Only 1011 days
But what if none of this ever happened?
What if instead of starving myself I starved my self-hatred?
My distortions would become smaller while my heart got
bigger
What if instead of burning fat I burned negativity?
My love would overpower the negative thoughts residing in
my brain
What if instead of counting calories I counted blessings?
I could appreciate every wonder in the world that filled my
brain instead of how many grams of fat are in low-fat butter
What if instead of purging meals I purged guilt?
Everything would be okay, and maybe then I'd be allowed
to use the bathroom after meals
Though now this is not the reality, it is now a distant image
in my mind
This new lifestyle shall soon be mine

The First Time

The first time I thought about my weight I was 9 years old
I stood in the mirror and looked at my innocent body
Instead of seeing the legs that carried me on adventures and
eyes that saw the world
I saw a round stomach and too thick arms
My hatred for myself began to flourish and my joy began to
fall
The first time I tried to diet I was 10 years old
Nobody noticed, and that was the worst part
Instead of enjoying ice cream and exotic tastes
I fed myself only water and celery
Hoping all this weight would go away
The number went down and I felt a sort of adrenaline that
I'd never felt before
The first time I tried body checking I was 10.5 years old
My friend began to speak about using her hands to measure
the width of her body
Instead of measuring love, I was measuring how thick my
fat was with hands that should have been holding those of
others
The first time I restricted I was 11 years old
After a comment that pierced my heart and destroyed my
pride
I would sit in front of the scale and sob when the number
didn't go down
I felt so lost and afraid of who I'd become
The first time I began to exercise obsessively I was 12 years
old
I would wake up before school and work out until my
muscles couldn't take it anymore

But to me, the pain was worth it for every single tenth of a
pound lost
The first time I purged I was 13 years old
I locked the bathroom door and stared at my reflection
You have to do this, I said
So you can look like them, I said
Fingers that should've been picking others up off the
ground were instead shoved down my throat
The first time I'd rather give up than gain weight I was 14
years old
Every time a pound came off, so did my will
Never once did anyone know my feelings were that
tremendous
My pale face and dark circles never told me otherwise
The first time I had hope for my future was on February 1st
It was the first day back from the hospital
I felt as if I could accomplish so much in my already
experienced life
Now I know that even in the darkest days, there was a light
ahead
And there shall be, as long as the earth turns and as long as
my lungs take in air
My hope will always be there

To My Sister

Dearest Lillian,

my love, there are many things you don't know
no amount of wisdom will be able to save you from this
cruel world in which we inhabit
it is with such displeasure that I write this, knowing that
you are only a tender 9 years old but you must listen
Number one: our society will try to teach you to hate
yourself, but you must be stronger
it will tell you to lose weight or go under the knife but with
great assurance I tell you that you must be content with who
you are, not who you think you should be
Number two: diet culture is not a lifestyle
It's a parasite that super models implant into your brain to
put you into self-destruction mode
No tenth of a pound is worth more than your happiness
Number three: you will be told that you cannot do the same
as men just because of the box checked on your birth
certificate
You are capable of anything that any man has the power to
achieve
People will tell you otherwise, but the most important thing
you may do is stay true to your pure identity
Number four: never trust anyone
never trust that guy you go to the bar with who keeps
buying you drinks
never trust that friend who pressures you to give up your
greatest secret
never trust the voice in your head telling you that you are
not worth it

because lily, the sad truth is that they will take advantage of
you
Number five: you control your future
Follow your dreams, no matter how impossible they seem
They will tell you that you cannot be the president, so go for
it
They will tell you that no man will ever love you; prove
them wrong
They will tell you that there's no point in trying to get that
promotion; go ahead and snatch you
So dear one, I may not be a genius, but I do have intelligence
that radiates inside me
In your long life, many challenges may be
but you are capable of much more than you can see

FREE VERSE

New Beginnings

new beginnings, a new era
a time to develop from not only lying on this fallen ground,
but climbing this mountain called life
to flourish is to live
as each breath is a step in the right direction
so in this coming day, allow yourself to grow
and be free in this birthed stay
on the planet where we reside
and new beginnings shall rise

Failure's Tone

failure
it's a word that's so feared yet nobody knows the true
meaning
it's a word that society uses to hang over top of your self-
worth
it's a word that makes you feel like your world is nothing
but grades and performance
like you're just a doll strapped into this roller coaster we call
life
but what is failure?
is it getting a 70 on an exam you were so sure you'd ace?
is it making jv instead of varsity even after you'd practiced
every day until you just couldn't take it anymore?
or is it the fear that you'll disappoint your parents because
you are not that perfect specimen they want you to be?
you are not a failure, nor will you ever be
your performance and experiences do not define you
think more of your successes instead of dwelling on failures
a number is only a number; a spot is only a spot
you are worth so much more and I promise that you shall go
far

I Love You

I love you
maybe not every little thing
no, you're not perfect, but that's not meant to be
the way you get excited every time you see hand lotion in a
store
the way you look at others through their own eyes
the way you never stop fighting even when the world turns
against you
your strength and compassion overrule your insecurity and
fear
this planet is so lucky to have you living here
your beauty comes from your heart, from the way you
always lift others up even when you're down
the world will never care what size pants you wear, but
instead the size of your dreams and the lack of your despair
miss lorelai, I promise, the world is rooting for you forever
and always
I beg you to love yourself as others do to you
Because you are a shining star and you must let your light
shine through

Life Is Too Short

life is too short
to spend your days staring at your body
criticizing every curve and edge
wishing them to just disappear
you are more than your weight
go out and live
walk among the flowers
and sing into a field
life is too short
so just breathe

The Rising of the Sun

life is too short
to spend your days staring at your body
criticizing every curve and edge
wishing them to just disappear
you are more than your weight
go out and live
walk among the flowers
and sing into a field
life is too short
so just breathe

Before

please don't go back to before
with lifeless eyes
and a sunken soul
please don't go back when your life was nothing more
than tears cried over the phone
begging for them to take you home
please don't go back to that day
when my perfect person was taken away
for far too long
every second I need you here
for a laugh, for a cheer
so please I beg of you, don't go back to before

True Beauty

there is nothing beautiful
about being unable to lie on your stomach
because your hip bones pierce through your skin
there is nothing beautiful
about waking up to find your hair laying in clumps on your
pillow
or not being able to shop at normal stores
because each size 0 pants falls down your rail thin legs
there is nothing beautiful about feeling like you're freezing
from the inside out
when it's over 50 degrees
what is beautiful
is loving yourself
treasuring every inch
and treating it as one shall treat a diamond
you are worth it
and you are beautiful

Beauty Is Pain

beautiful
our society tells us that we must
have a small waist and slim hips
but you must not be too skinny
or have too many rolls
because beauty is measured in numbers
your measurements cannot be too high
and your weight must not tip the scale
you are worth more than a number
that number does not validate you
your true beauty comes from within
no matter what, you will be beautiful
starlight comes from you, love
look at society and just let go
you are who you are meant to be
not someone else, not me
now go on, and change the world
my belief lives in you
fix your crown and push through

Breath of Life

the reason I breathe
is you
your love overpowers the hate
the hate that is slowly killing me
please, stay here
I need you here
forever and ever

The Connotation of Health

you look healthy
it stings; it burns
every time I hear those words
my heart falls
but my dear, healthy does not mean fat
it means you've gained the light in your eyes back
and your collarbones don't look as if they'll leave your skin
you were made to inspire
words do hurt, but you have the control
the control of how you let them manipulate your precious
mind
before you let your thoughts overpower you
step back, and focus
focus once again

My Love for You

my love for you
radiates as the ocean spreads across the sand
it grows and grows
as a flower's stem sprouts

Hold On

don't let go
your slim fingers hold the rope
the rope that leads to the path of righteousness
along the gardens of love and the fields of strength
there is not but one reason that you are here
it is that you hold the will to push through
as the mountains climb and the hills roll
she begs of you to stay still
and allow yourself to live
among this beautiful planet made for you

Ana's Validation

your validity is not determined
by your lowest weight
or the space between your thighs
it is not determined by how many times you have been
hospitalized
or how low your heart rate reached
it is determined by you being you
and every beautiful characteristic that you engulf
just by living, you are valid
that is the way it always shall be

Hope

have hope
this pain shall end
the skies will open
and cleanse will come
saving you from the current misery
that may be present, but it is not the future
walk along into the breeze
carrying you to better days

Day by Day

there are days when you feel on cloud nine
and others where you are trapped in a fiery hell
ups and downs
back and forth
the earth still turns
no matter where you stand
the sun will shine
behind the thick cloud covers
the ocean will flow
capturing you in its embrace
to bring you to a warmer place

Little Things

the littlest things
may hold so much meaning
that the littlest flicker of light
may brighten the entire palace
and that little flicker
may be the beginning
of something beautiful
and something grand

You

there are times
where hope may all seem lost
yet there are times
when every little puzzle piece seems to fall together
in these times so different, you are the same person
your feelings do not define you
nor do they shape you
in every breathing second, you are you

The Treasure of You

your strength may move mountains
and your voice can shape the sea
the will you carry may change the world
and your hope forever shines
there is not one day not made for you
the universe turns
and the stars glow
for this will always be true
the world is not complete without your continued breath
so please keep fighting
and never let go
of this treasured life you hold

The World in Your Hands

you deserve the world, my angel
all of the riches and diamonds
that one may provide
should be given as the gratitude for your mind

Your Precious Breath

life is tough
as are you
no incident in the world
shall ever be grand enough to take life away from your
breathing body
it is worth it, I swear
you may not see it now
but that does not mean it is not there

The House That Made You

your body is a home
to all things inside
your heart that flutters when you see one whom you love
your stomach that holds all of the food consumed on your
adventures
your brain that consists of every beautiful trait that makes
up who you are
every cell
no matter how big or how small
is important, as it is the beautiful creature who has been
there through it all

A Stainless Steel Heart

her mind is as strong as stainless steel
yet as delicate as a feather
it is as precious as rubies
and as rare as gold
it buds creativity
and bleeds grace

His Words

his steel sword
stabs into my weak heart
as blood rushes out
the last love for myself gushes
he is now a part of me
holding, grasping
I wretch in pain
only to be left scarred and alone

A Glimmer of Hope

a glimmer of hope
a sparkle of wisdom
together we stand
together at last
this shall be
the true beginning
of what shall exist forevermore

Together

do not look to heal
on your own
look at the presence of others
who may assist you in this reconciliation

The Heart Wants What it Wants

the heart wants what it wants
listen to the faint beat
thumping over and over
look where it points
and follow

My Body's Welcome

body, I want to be your friend
thank you, she whispered
it is about time
after long years, a victory was won

Sick Enough

there is no such thing as sick enough
sick is not a beautiful thing
nor shall it be celebrated
it is a disease
a pained parasite
who takes the breath from the host in which it resides

Pride

be proud of how far you have come
as many could not have done what you have

Time of Life

it may take time
to figure out life
no book ends in a split second
have patience
and let reality take its toll

Ana's Wrath

a woman among a masquerade
sly and quick, but never alone
grasping onto the weakest
taking the will from the strongest
Ana kills, but never loves

The Flight of Growth

like a butterfly you must grow
this growth will bring new beginnings
a change that will save your being
and take you forward, flying through life

Free Flight

you are a bird
free and beautiful
your wings are gold
your eyes are amber

A New Place

fly away, dear one
leave your troubles behind
welcome yourself into a new land
of peace and tranquility
hatred and injustice will flourish no more
in this land of love and cherished hope

The Past Is in the Past

look how far you've come
still living, still breathing
despite all of the trauma and all of the pain

Escaping the War

but I want to live
not in constant battle
with my mind and my heart
never knowing which side to choose
it's a sort of carnage
though only to one's self

Hope Chooses Hope

there's hope for all, but hope for none
as even hope chooses victims
victims who are mangled by its claws
and left for dead
fear not, my love
this is only fiction
pay attention to the diction
and love yourself forevermore
you deserve to be content and lay to rest
the churning in your head

Love Is a Suicide Note

love is a suicide note
asking for pain
slowly manipulating you and driving you insane
it abruptly ends, leaving you alone
alone with your thoughts
but you must pick yourself up
and build off yourself
not letting this be the end of your

You Before Him

you were an angel
and he was common folk
he could not cope with your perfection
the way your smile glows
and your hair flows
you will never not be enough for him
it was that you were too much

The Truth of Starvation

her eyelids flutter
her heart rate falls
bones jut out and pain shoots up
starvation seems like the only option
yet it is the true enemy
malnourishment won't solve your problems
it'll only halt them until they are too large to solve them

When it Hit

happiness hit me
the sadness flooded out
the seas were parted
as I walked down this pathway called life
this time it was real
not hidden with a mask
the feeling is true
overwhelming me, saving me
let it stay
among me, with me

Homosapiens

isn't it beautiful
how much diversity there is in one species
how the patterns that trace our bodies
have their own unique print
and though our composition is the same
it presents itself so differently

True Worth

you are worthy
no matter the number flashed on the scale
you are valued
no matter how high your jean size is
you are enough
no matter how your hands wrap around your waist
your being is so much more than your body
your body, it's foundation of life, is your being

The Middle

stuck in the middle
in between hell and heaven
unaware of where to go
the easiest option may not be grand
continue forward
though challenges may arrive
this too shall pass

The Power of Her Rays

you have come too far to let go now
bloom from the darkness
grow from the pain
let the sun's rays empower you
arise each day

Life as a Novel

life flows as the ink from a pen
experiences are stories
feelings are components
there are conflicts and downfalls
written across every page of the novel
yet a resolution will come
ending with peace and content

Freedom at Last

you have come so far
leaving the past behind
climbing the mountains of gold
leading yourself to what the future holds
the time has come where the war is won
let the bells ring
let me be free

When I was Younger

when I was younger, I looked at the world like a
kaleidoscope
full of magic, full of colors
always on my side
hand-in-hand I walked through life
with this fantasy, held so dearly without an outside thought
as I grew older, the rainbow turned to gray
the flowers turned to dust
the buildings crumbled and the magic fell
I was left alone, with no hand to hold

Blooming Beyond

growing frantically from the gentle soil
upwards towards the sun the wildflowers toil
stems reaching up and roots that coil
petals glide and honeydew lays
on the tiny shells, soft as foil
from these stunned organisms radiate
bits of iridescence

at this point, I question
is it worth it?
the pain and twisted games
the wheels turning in my brain
the weight has stayed; the hope has grown
every day I sit in fear
feeling like a stranger in my own body
recovery is far from easy
it is tedious
agonizing
holding me down
restraining my will
I am stronger
I will not let go
the light floats farther
I pick myself up; I step back
this is possible
for I shall live this way no more
the cuffs are unlocked; the restraints are broken
my soul ever lasts
it is so close
I reach and reach
then finally, recovery is in my fingertips

I am hungry
hungry for life
a life to live freely
not held down by the chains spewed from my mind
bringing hope down, and debilitating the will to breathe
my desire is to go out and soar
among the wonders of the world
that our world holds in store
open the doors

I was hiding for so long
alienating myself from reality
with the fear in my heart and the pain in my mind
telling me to stop and let it die
the day is new, and the time is right
let it be risen into the light
open the doors; the palace will fill
no more longer this journey downhill
hold it still; the photos are taken
for I am here, no longer hiding
not a fear, not a worry
this body is fine and forever it shall be
the true protector surrounding me

The Blooming of My Soul

bloom as a sunflower
allow your core to collect the rays
as your petals pause the daze
brought from inside and held as one
your constant friend will be the sun
take care of what you have
one day it may all be gone
leaving the power in the hands
attached to your body, created by men
focus on now
today may be your last
what you know will be the past

Drink Up

drink hope from glasses
sip strength from mugs
ground yourself in the moonlight
and lift your mind to the sun
let your lungs take in radiance
and heart pump power
your eyes will see freedom
your ears will hear joy
for the world is in your hands
who will embrace the future
and encapsulate every living day

Scars to Your Beautiful

don't hide my love
your scars show strength that will forever be
trapped inside your innocent heart
a heart that loves others yet cannot bear to love themselves
if only they saw how beautiful they were
when their face lights up on a sunny day
and the way they dance around the room
having so much to say
the war is not yet won but each battle comes out to be
an internal victory leading a path
to self-love forevermore

The Curse of Literature

they will try to bury you
suffocating your breath
their words are daggers
their looks are bayonets
you have one weapon they don't: your mind
use the flow of the words to pin them down
the metaphors will curse them
the similes will kill
literature is the tactic only few shall have

Measured Beauty

beauty comes from within
instead of the size of your waist
it is the size of your heart
the compassion you hold for others
and the love treasured inside
every breath you take radiates your beauty
and spreads joy throughout this hateful planet
you can be the change in showing true beauty
love yourself, for you are the only you there is

For You

the stars shine for you
their light stealing what's gone
bringing it back to life
taking the hatred you hold
stealing your sorrows away
letting it become something new
a feeling too grand to overwhelm
that will save what is lost
making it forever found

Break the Chains

you cannot allow yourself to become a hostage to your brain
your thoughts hold you at gunpoint
your feelings chain you up
use the words to unlock the cuffs
your strength inside shall forever be enough
to end this hell
burning inside of this young precious mind

Racing

thoughts of you
raced my mind
your precious soul
always behind
the pain inside
that screamed and cried
Longing to be released
with strength and pride

Lie

he lies
his words caress your hope
to feel like the one you want to be
but it's false
only a dream and despair

She, the Sun

you are the sun
your hair, its rays
your eyes, its heat

Finally

my whole life I have waited for this
a chance to be seen
for my battles to be recognized

Change by Day

from one split second to another
from a thin girl in a hospital bed to colorful words erupting
in my head

My Epiphany

but I want to live
not in constant battle
with my mind and my heart
never knowing which side to choose
it's a sort of carnage
though only to one's self

From That Moment On

the moment I saw you
the arson in my heart was ignited
the ammunition in my eyes was sparked
your amber eyes captivated my soul
and your smile regained my peace
it pulls me down slowly
caressing my love
holding my strength
encapsulating my being
forever and ever again

Love Doesn't Discriminate

love doesn't discriminate
nor pick and choose
scanning the blood on your conscience
pinning down your past
it grabs the innocent ones
who are living past their destined life
hoping so lightly for someone
someone to scoop them up
bringing them to a forgotten land

In and Out

breathe in; breathe out
ashes fall; sadness calls
minds chase endless worry
anxiety, anxiety please hurry
never able to leave me alone
please, I beg you, you've already shown
the pain you cause is utterly surreal
each night I think of what I feel
my life is complicated without you here
but you are a parasite
you need room to grow
as I myself do as well

The Drug That's You

your eyes captivate me
your words, they shake me
building cathedrals after every comma
skyscrapers from every sentence
your pure presence alleviates me
from the pain and agony inside
you are my drug, the one that cures me
from this living hell burning inside this gentle child's mind

Anxiety, Anxiety

let me breathe, please
you're suffocating me
drowning me
in an ocean of despair
swarmed by winds of anger and rage
anxiety, please, please
let me live in peace
without you holding me back, surrounding me
leave me be

Stainless Steel Hearts

let the rain wash away
the sorrows and pain from yesterday
stand up straight and face it on
don't hide behind this mask you wear
for you are beautiful
you are strong
this battle you have fought for so long
will be won, not with a rifle
but with your stainless steel heart inside

Here

I hope to be content
Within my own true self
To love and cherish who I am
Without a blocking hand

I stand up for what I believe
No matter the cost at stake
For I know what is right and wrong
And will not sit another day

I love others as they love me
My heart beats for those who surround me
Though I loathe to give up
I shall never stop fighting

Strength is real; strength is there
It resides in me and will continue
As long as I live and when
I am here

Growth from Light

the wind will capture you
raise you up
your arms are lifted by the heavens above
let it fall down to the earth
sinking, straining into the nourished soil

Safety Stays

you have nothing to fear
the skies have closed
the ocean halts
for grace and strength are here

Beauty from Above

don't be beautiful like her; be beautiful like you
your hair cascades
your eyelids flutter
your skin shines like the brightest stars
she is her; you are you
she is beautiful, as are you

Away

his hatred isn't love
he has hurt you
don't let him stay
fly through the air
far, far away

She Stayed

when everyone has fled
leaving you alone, in pain
in a ditch of despair and loss
your body was here
despite it all
she stayed

The Someone

don't just look for someone
look for a person who captures your heart
and makes your happiness rocket sky high
choose him for being everyone to your lively heart
not just for being someone

Devotions Deserved

you deserve love
not to feel alone and disregarded
but to feel the radiance from others
that brings you forward

Starving Dreams

a dream is not deserved
it is reserved for the time when you needed it most
do not sacrifice yourself to be someone who you aren't
feed your little girl spirit to make this dream come alive

Home of the Soul

every human deserves a home
no human deserves to be alone
do not only feed their hunger — feed their dreams that
bring them forward
do not only quench their thirst — quench the fear for this
world
a human brain is the most powerful of all
leave it plain, or let it roar

You Before Them

fall in love with yourself before any other being
you shall have yourself for life
put that first before becoming a stranger's wife
don't sell your love to an enriched king
hold it tight, and save your hand
for one whose love is greater than the strength of any man

Cracks Are Not Permanent

you are not broken
just cracked
you will heal with time
let the sun and her power seal the crack
that vibrates in your heart
it may shape you
but it will not break you
one day at a time, you will be
one day at a time, you shall see

The End of It All

my heart was stolen from my chest
by a girl with willowy arms and a broken soul
whose spidery fingers grasped my mind
a puppeteer she became to me
leaving only darkness in this pitch-black world
her rail legs sitting on the earth
round and round it turns
slowly fading away
leaving dust as the only existence to stay

What Is Love?

love shouldn't be a chore
we should rise each day and see the light
cast by the rainbows
holding excitement for this new time
where the one for us is out there
waiting with open arms

The Elements

he was a fire
always asking for more
hesitant to let go
you were an ocean
gentle and soft among the world
holding enough power to drown his dismay

Our Society

they come so fast
holding promises to their chest
yet we live in a society of dull propriety
that they grab what they desire
and escape with the wind
thinking nothing
as this is the norm
set for us by the past
why not make a new future
in which our broken hearts are sewn together
leading to prosperous and admired love

Grateful

it is so simple to hate what we have
we do not look around
to see the mountains of gold and the seas of silver
that protect us
no matter the money in our pocket or the clothes on our
back
riches do not determine value
your life determines value
your lungs taking in air
your heart thumping in your chest
that value comes from inside

Death of a Friend

you were supposed to be a friend
a person who held me tight during a rainstorm
yet you were the rainstorm
whose waters knocked me off my feet
whose winds brought the breath from inside my chest
you took the best from me
left me stranded alone
on an island of fear and hateful memories